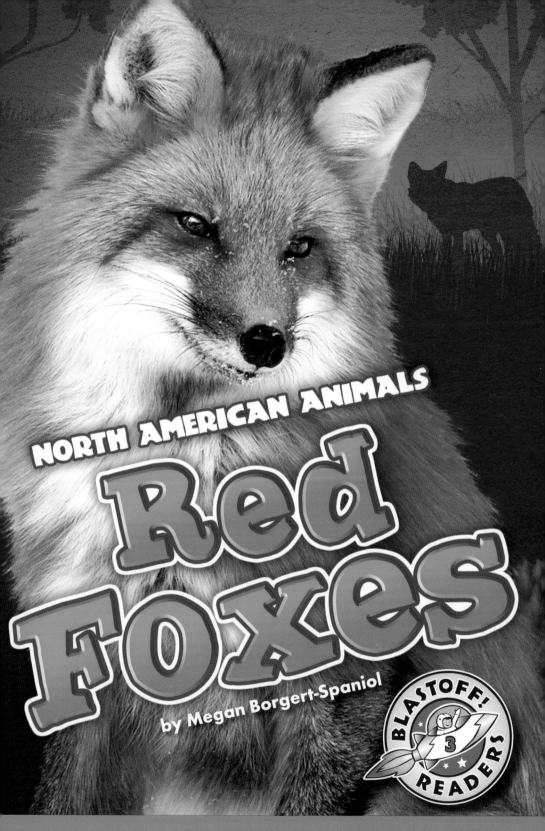

NORTH AMERICAN ANIMALS

Red Foxes

by Megan Borgert-Spaniol

BELLWETHER MEDIA • MINNEAPOLIS, MN

Note to Librarians, Teachers, and Parents:

Blastoff! Readers are carefully developed by literacy experts and combine standards-based content with developmentally appropriate text.

Level 1 provides the most support through repetition of high-frequency words, light text, predictable sentence patterns, and strong visual support.

Level 2 offers early readers a bit more challenge through varied simple sentences, increased text load, and less repetition of high-frequency words.

Level 3 advances early-fluent readers toward fluency through increased text and concept load, less reliance on visuals, longer sentences, and more literary language.

Level 4 builds reading stamina by providing more text per page, increased use of punctuation, greater variation in sentence patterns, and increasingly challenging vocabulary.

Level 5 encourages children to move from "learning to read" to "reading to learn" by providing even more text, varied writing styles, and less familiar topics.

Whichever book is right for your reader, Blastoff! Readers are the perfect books to build confidence and encourage a love of reading that will last a lifetime!

This edition first published in 2015 by Bellwether Media, Inc.

No part of this publication may be reproduced in whole or in part without written permission of the publisher. For information regarding permission, write to Bellwether Media, Inc., Attention: Permissions Department, 5357 Penn Avenue South, Minneapolis, MN 55419.

Library of Congress Cataloging-in-Publication Data

Borgert-Spaniol, Megan, 1989-
   Red Foxes / by Megan Borgert-Spaniol.
      pages cm. – (Blastoff! Readers. North American Animals)
   Includes bibliographical references and index.
   Summary: "Simple text and full-color photography introduce beginning readers to red foxes. Developed by literacy experts for students in kindergarten through third grade"– Provided by publisher.
   Audience: Ages 5-8.
   Audience: K to Grade 3.
   ISBN 978-1-62617-193-0 (hardcover : alk. paper)
   1. Red fox–Juvenile literature. I. Title.
   QL737.C22B62 2015
   599.775–dc23
                              2014037323

Table of **Contents**

What Are Red Foxes?

Red foxes are **mammals** that belong to the dog family.

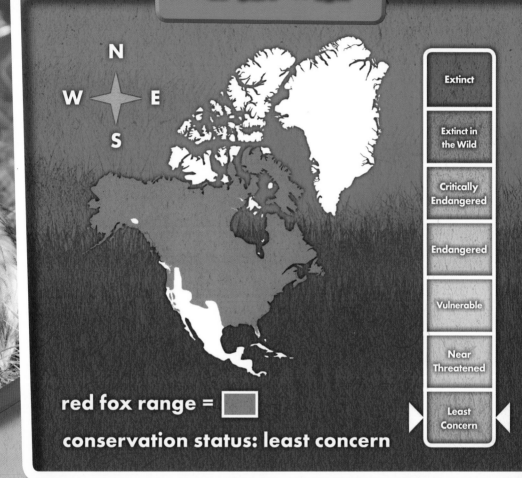

N
W · E
S

Extinct

Extinct in the Wild

Critically Endangered

Endangered

Vulnerable

Near Threatened

Least Concern

red fox range = ▢

conservation status: least concern

They can be found throughout most of the United States and Canada.

These foxes can **adapt** to many different **habitats**. They live in forests, deserts, and grasslands.

Some even make homes
around farms and city parks.

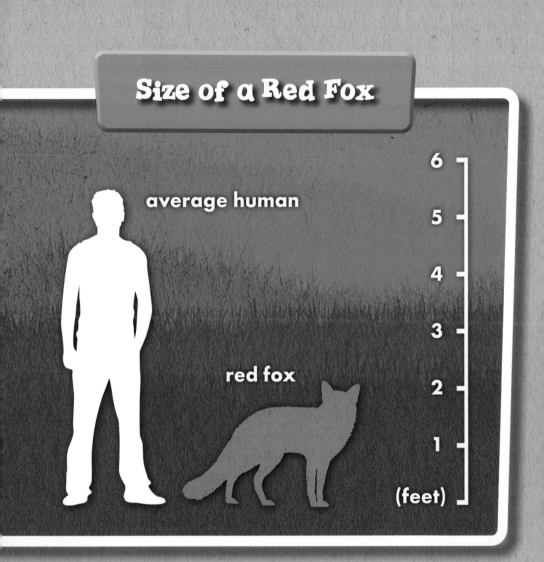

Size of a Red Fox

average human

red fox

6
5
4
3
2
1
(feet)

Red foxes are the largest kind of fox. They are the size of a small dog. They usually weigh 10 to 15 pounds (4.5 to 6.8 kilograms).

Most have red-orange fur down their backs and sides. Some have silver, black, or reddish brown fur. All red foxes have black legs and black ear tips.

Bushy Tails

Red foxes have long, bushy tails with white tips.

Identify a Red Fox

tail with white tip

black legs

pointed ears with black tips

The tips set red foxes apart from gray foxes. Their tails have black tips.

Red foxes use their
tails to balance
when they move.

They also curl up under
their tails in cold weather.

Finding Food

Red foxes are **omnivores**. They hunt for mice, rabbits, and birds. They also eat insects, fruits, and **carrion**.

deer mice

cottontail rabbits

ring-necked pheasants

red-legged grasshoppers

apples

sunflower seeds

Sometimes they take food from garbage cans and farms.

These foxes stand still to listen and watch for **prey**. Then they leap at their meal and trap it under their front paws.

They bury any extra food under leaves or snow.

Caring for Pups

A female red fox gives birth to up to 12 **pups**. The **newborns** have gray-brown fur. They live in a **den** built by their mom.

Baby Facts

Name for babies: pups or kits

Size of litter: 4 to 6 pups (most common)

Length of pregnancy: about 7 weeks

Time spent with mom: about 7 months

The pups begin to play outside
after about a month.

Their parents bring them live prey to eat. This helps the pups learn how to hunt!

Glossary

adapt—to become comfortable with something

carrion—the rotting meat of a dead animal

den—a sheltered place; red foxes make their dens out of holes in the ground.

habitats—lands with certain types of plants, animals, and weather

mammals—warm-blooded animals that have backbones and feed their young milk

newborns—babies that were just recently born

omnivores—animals that eat both plants and animals

prey—animals that are hunted by other animals for food

pups—baby red foxes; kit is another name for a baby red fox.

To Learn More

AT THE LIBRARY

Banks, Kate. *Fox.* New York, N.Y.: Farrar, Straus and Giroux, 2007.

Hollenbeck, Kathleen M. *Red Fox at Hickory Lane.* Norwalk, Conn.: Soundprints, 2004.

Johnson, J. Angelique. *Red Foxes.* Mankato, Minn.: Capstone Press, 2011.

ON THE WEB

Learning more about red foxes is as easy as 1, 2, 3.

1. Go to www.factsurfer.com.

2. Enter "red foxes" into the search box.

3. Click the "Surf" button and you will see a list of related web sites.

With factsurfer.com, finding more information is just a click away.

Index

The images in this book are reproduced through the courtesy of: Geoffrey Kuchera, front cover; Radius Images/ Corbis, pp. 4-5; Minden Pictures/ SuperStock, p. 6; Paul Reeves Photography, pp. 6-7, 15 (bottom left); Michael Quinton, p. 9; Menno Schaefer, pp. 10-11; James E. Seward, p. 11 (top left); Jeannette Katzir Photog, p. 11 (top center); Richard Guijt Photography, p. 11 (top right); Eric Isselee, p. 11 (bottom); Pim Leijen, p. 12; Michael Cummings/ Getty Images, pp. 12-13; Graham Manson/ Getty Images, pp. 14-15; Close Encounters Photo, p. 15 (top left); Vaclav Volrab, p. 15 (top right); Tom Reicher, p. 15 (middle left); Maria Jeffs, p. 15 (middle right); bergamont, p. 15 (bottom right); Barrett Hedges/ Getty Images, p. 16; JKlingebiel, p. 17; Jürgen & Christine Sohns/ Glow Images, pp. 18-19; Joakim Stolt, p. 19; Don Johnston/ Glow Images, p. 20; Gerard Lacz Images/ SuperStock, p. 21.